First World War
and Army of Occupation
War Diary
France, Belgium and Germany

59 DIVISION
Divisional Troops
469 Field Company Royal Engineers
17 February 1917 - 16 July 1919

WO95/3017/4

Published by

The Naval & Military Press Ltd

Unit 10 Ridgewood Industrial Park,

Uckfield, East Sussex,

TN22 5QE England

Tel: +44 (0) 1825 749494

www.naval-military-press.com

www.nmarchive.com

This diary has been reprinted in facsimile from the original. Any imperfections are inevitably reproduced and the quality may fall short of modern type and cartographic standards.

© Crown Copyright

Images reproduced by permission of The N

Contents

Document type	Place/Title	Date From	Date To
Heading	WO95/3017/4		
Heading	59th Division 469th Field Coy R.E. Feb 1917-July 1919		
War Diary	Lark Hill	17/02/1917	17/02/1917
War Diary	Southampton	17/02/1917	21/02/1917
War Diary	Le Harve	24/02/1917	25/02/1917
War Diary	Longeau	26/02/1917	26/02/1917
War Diary	Glisy	27/02/1917	27/02/1917
War Diary	Bayon Villers	28/02/1917	28/02/1917
War Diary	Estrees	02/03/1917	02/03/1917
War Diary	Bayonvillers	04/03/1917	04/03/1917
War Diary	Estrees	08/03/1917	18/03/1917
War Diary	St Christ	19/03/1917	19/03/1917
War Diary	Eterpigny	26/03/1917	26/03/1917
War Diary	Boucly Beaumetz	28/03/1917	28/03/1917
War Diary	Bouvincourt	01/04/1917	05/04/1917
War Diary	Boucly	06/04/1917	10/04/1917
War Diary	Roisel	10/04/1917	10/04/1917
War Diary	Hesbecourt	14/04/1917	14/04/1917
War Diary	Roisel	14/04/1917	14/04/1917
War Diary	Templeux	18/04/1917	30/04/1917
War Diary	Hesbecourt	30/04/1917	30/04/1917
War Diary	Roisel	10/04/1917	24/05/1917
War Diary	Neuville	24/05/1917	05/07/1917
War Diary	Barastre	06/07/1917	31/07/1917
War Diary	Le Transloy	27/07/1917	27/07/1917
War Diary	Barastre	01/08/1917	15/08/1917
War Diary	Millencourt	22/08/1917	01/09/1917
War Diary	Proven	01/09/1917	01/09/1917
War Diary	Oudizeele	02/09/1917	04/09/1917
War Diary	Poperinghe	04/09/1917	22/09/1917
War Diary	Ypres	23/09/1917	30/09/1917
War Diary	Vlamertinghe	30/09/1917	30/09/1917
War Diary	Ypres	30/09/1917	30/09/1917
War Diary	Vlamertinghe	30/09/1917	01/10/1917
War Diary	Watou	02/10/1917	02/10/1917
War Diary	Seaton Camp	02/10/1917	04/10/1917
War Diary	Thiennes	05/10/1917	06/10/1917
War Diary	Cuhem	07/10/1917	10/10/1917
War Diary	Dieval	11/10/1917	11/10/1917
War Diary	Maisnil-Les-Ruitz	12/10/1917	12/10/1917
War Diary	Vancouver Camp	13/10/1917	13/10/1917
War Diary	Avion Sector	17/10/1917	18/10/1917
War Diary	Ablain St Nazaire	19/10/1917	22/10/1917
War Diary	Avion Sector	23/10/1917	23/10/1917
War Diary	Houchin	24/10/1917	24/10/1917
War Diary	Avion Sector	30/10/1917	17/11/1917
War Diary	Ablain St Nazaire	19/11/1917	19/11/1917
War Diary	Gouy En A	20/11/1917	20/11/1917
War Diary	Ransart	22/11/1917	22/11/1917
War Diary	Achiet Le Petit	23/11/1917	23/11/1917

War Diary	Dessart Wood	26/11/1917	26/11/1917
War Diary	Trescault	28/11/1917	29/11/1917
War Diary	Flesquieres	01/12/1917	10/12/1917
War Diary	Grand Ravine	10/12/1917	10/12/1917
War Diary	Flesquieres	10/12/1917	23/12/1917
War Diary	Rocquigny	23/12/1917	24/12/1917
War Diary	Neuville	20/12/1917	20/12/1917
War Diary	Rocquigny	25/12/1917	25/12/1917
War Diary	Sars Le Bois	25/12/1917	31/12/1917
War Diary	Rebreuviette	01/01/1918	29/01/1918
War Diary	Berles-Au-Bois	30/01/1918	30/01/1918
War Diary	Ervillers	31/01/1918	31/01/1918
War Diary	Rebreuviette	01/01/1918	26/01/1918
War Diary	Ervillers	01/02/1918	09/02/1918
War Diary	Mory	09/02/1918	18/02/1918
War Diary	Bullecourt	18/02/1918	18/02/1918
War Diary	Mory	22/02/1918	23/02/1918
War Diary	Bullecourt	11/02/1918	28/02/1918
Heading	59th Divisional Engineers 469th Field Company R.E. March 1918		
War Diary	Ecoust	01/03/1918	21/03/1918
War Diary	Mory	05/03/1918	12/03/1918
War Diary	Ecoust	18/03/1918	21/03/1918
War Diary	Bullecourt	21/03/1918	21/03/1918
War Diary	Ervillers	22/03/1918	22/03/1918
War Diary	Mory	21/03/1918	21/03/1918
War Diary	Ervillers	22/03/1918	22/03/1918
War Diary	Ayette	23/03/1918	23/03/1918
War Diary	Aveluy	25/03/1918	25/03/1918
War Diary	Pont Noyelles	26/03/1918	26/03/1918
War Diary	Montrelet	28/03/1918	28/03/1918
War Diary	Lapuonoy	28/03/1918	28/03/1918
War Diary	Maisnil St Pol	29/03/1918	29/03/1918
War Diary	Frevillers	29/03/1918	29/03/1918
War Diary	Bethonsart	29/03/1918	31/03/1918
Heading	59th Divisional Engineers 469th Field Company R.E. April 1918		
War Diary	St Janter Biezen	01/04/1918	03/04/1918
War Diary	Ypres	04/04/1918	12/04/1918
War Diary	Brandhoek	13/04/1918	13/04/1918
War Diary	Godewaersvelde	14/04/1918	14/04/1918
War Diary	Locre	16/04/1918	19/04/1918
War Diary	Reninghelst	20/04/1918	20/04/1918
War Diary	Elverdinghe	21/04/1918	21/04/1918
War Diary	Watou	22/04/1918	27/04/1918
War Diary	St Jan Ter Biezen	29/04/1918	29/04/1918
War Diary	Poperinghe	30/04/1918	06/05/1918
War Diary	Houtkerque	07/05/1918	07/05/1918
War Diary	St Omer	09/05/1918	09/05/1918
War Diary	Cauchie D Ecques	10/05/1918	10/05/1918
War Diary	Sachin	11/05/1918	11/05/1918
War Diary	Houdain	12/05/1918	21/05/1918
War Diary	Febvin Palfort	22/05/1918	22/05/1918
War Diary	Clarques	23/05/1918	29/06/1918
War Diary	Clarques & Bilques	01/06/1918	30/06/1918
War Diary	Clarques	03/07/1918	03/07/1918

War Diary	Bilques	05/07/1918	05/07/1918
War Diary	Clarques	06/07/1918	06/07/1918
War Diary	Bilques	08/07/1918	08/07/1918
War Diary	Clarques	09/07/1918	23/07/1918
War Diary	Fontaines-Lez-Boulans	24/07/1918	24/07/1918
War Diary	Bellacourt	30/07/1918	30/07/1918
War Diary	Clarques & Bilques	01/07/1918	22/07/1918
War Diary	Bellacourt	01/08/1918	23/08/1918
War Diary	Saulty	24/08/1918	24/08/1918
War Diary	Aire	24/08/1918	24/08/1918
War Diary	St Quentin	27/08/1918	27/08/1918
War Diary	Robecq	28/08/1918	01/09/1918
War Diary	Fosse	01/09/1918	04/10/1918
War Diary	Bois Grenier	04/10/1918	17/10/1918
War Diary	St Helene (Lille)	20/10/1918	20/10/1918
War Diary	Templeuve	24/10/1918	10/11/1918
War Diary	Esquelmes	11/11/1918	15/11/1918
War Diary	Ainstaing	16/11/1918	16/11/1918
War Diary	Seclin	20/11/1918	04/12/1918
War Diary	Braquemont	05/12/1918	11/12/1918
War Diary	Ligny St Flochel	14/12/1918	28/12/1918
Heading	To D.A.G. G.H.Q. 31st Echelon I Herewith Enclose This Units War Diary For The Month Of January		
War Diary	Ligny St Flochel	01/01/1919	06/01/1919
War Diary	New Minx	01/01/1919	01/01/1919
War Diary	Noeux Le Minx	06/01/1919	06/01/1919
War Diary	Ligny St Flochel	07/01/1919	07/01/1919
War Diary	Dunkirk	08/01/1919	31/01/1919
War Diary	Mardyck Camp Dunkirk	01/02/1919	31/03/1919
War Diary	Dunkirk	01/06/1919	16/07/1919

WO 95
30171/4

59TH DIVISION

469TH FIELD COY. R.E.
FEB 1917 - ~~DEC 1918~~
JULY 1919

WAR DIARY or INTELLIGENCE SUMMARY

469th (N.M) FIELD Co R.E.

Army Form C. 2118.

(Erase heading not required.)

Instructions regarding War Diaries and Intelligence Summaries are contained in F. S. Regs., Part II. and the Staff Manual respectively. Title Pages will be prepared in manuscript.

Place	Date	Hour	Summary of Events and Information	Remarks and references to Appendices
K HILL	17.2.17	5.0 A.M.	Company with full transport entrained at AMESBURY Station	
		9.30	arrived SOUTHAMPTON	
		6.0 P.M.	Embarked on transport MANCHESTER IMPORTER.	
THAMPTON	19.2.17	11.0 A.M.	2 men taken off transport having contracted measles	
THAMPTON	20.2.17	3.0 P.M.	Transport put back to SOUTHAMPTON. Men disembarked & taken to Rest Camp	
			3 more men taken away with Measles	
	21.2.17	12.0 noon	Company re-embarked on MANCHESTER IMPORTER.	
ARVE	24.2.17	11.30 A.M.	Dis-embarked & marched to No.5 Rest Camp	
	25.2.17	9.0	2 more measles reported. These men came off at No.5 Rest Camp together with 21 men (Contact cases)	
	25.2.17		Entrained at No 3 Pier	
do	26.2.17	4.0 A.M.	Detrained & marched to GLISY.	
SY	27.2.17	9.0 A.M.	Marched to BAYONVILLERS	
NVILLERS	28.2.17	12 a noon	Advance Party of 1 Officer & 26 other ranks proceeded to N 20 c 38. Proceeded continued place attached to 446th FIELD Co R.E.	

M.R. [signature] Major
O/C 469th FIELD Co R.E.

Army Form C. 2118.

C. 2118. 469th Field C.R.E. from March 1st to March 30th 1917

WAR DIARY
or
INTELLIGENCE SUMMARY.
(Erase heading not required.)

Vol I

Instructions regarding War Diaries and Intelligence Summaries are contained in F.S. Regs., Part II. and the Staff Manual respectively. Title pages will be prepared in manuscript.

Hour, Date, Place	Summary of Events and Information	Remarks and references to Appendices
10 AM 2/3/17 ESTREES.	Advance party of C. 1 Officer & 26 other ranks left Hedgeauville of 446th Field Co. & proceeded to ESTREES to take over station from 447th Field Co.	
10 AM 4/3/17 BINIONVILLERS.	Company inspected by C.E. Army Corps	
10 AM 8/3/17 ESTREES.	Company moved to ESTREES from BAYONVILLERS. Minden Lantern generated FOUCAUCOURT.	
8/3/17 to 18/3/17 ESTREES.	Company employed in revetting & clearing C.T's & wiring reserve & preparing INTERMEDIATE LINE. (East of BERNY) for defence. One party at Trans. Wagon Lines East of BERNY. Company marched to ST CHRIST.	
19/3/17 ST CHRIST. A.M.	Company marched to ST CHRIST. Construction of BRIDGES across the Canal & River Somme for transport & foot infantry. Also employed on water supply MISERY & MAZANCOURT.	
10 AM 26/3/17 ETERPIGNY.	Company marched to ETERPIGNY. Work commenced on BRIDGE crossing Canal. Run SOMME & Marsh	
5 pm 28/3/17 BOUCLY BEAUMETZ	½ Company No 1 & 4 sections proceeded to BOUCLY & BEAUMETZ to assist 179th Brigade in making strong points & wiring defensive position	

Signed J. M. C.
Major R.E.
O/C 469

ORIGINAL 59

WAR DIARY
or
INTELLIGENCE SUMMARY

of the 469th FIELD Co R.E.
from April 1st to April 30th 1917.

Army Form C. 2118.

(Erase heading not required.)

Instructions regarding War Diaries and Intelligence Summaries are contained in F.S. Regs., Part II and the Staff Manual respectively. Title pages will be prepared in manuscript.

Hour, Date, Place		Summary of Events and Information	Remarks and references to Appendices
0 A.M.	1/4/17. BOUVINCOURT.	Company less Nos 1 & 4. Sections marched from ETERPIGNY to BOUVINCOURT.	1 of 3
	2/4/17 to 5/4/17. BOUVINCOURT.	Company principally employed on clearations of roads round craters in vicinity	
8 A.M.	6/4/17. BOUCLY.	Company less Nos 1 & 4. Sections marched to BOUCLY. went under (Canvas).	
	7/4/17. BOUCLY.	No 2. Section proceeded to ROISEL (attached to 177th Brigade)	
	7/4/17. BOUCLY.	No 1. Section returned to Co. Headquarters at BOUCLY.	
7/4/17 to 10/4/17 BOUCLY.		Company employed on clearations round craters.	
30 P.M.	10/4/17 ROISEL.	Company (less 2 & 4. Sections) marched to ROISEL	
	10/4/17. HESBECOURT.	No. 3 Section proceeded to HESBECOURT. (attached to 177th Brigade.	
	14/4/17 ROISEL.	No. 4 Section returned to Company Headquarters ROISEL	
	18/4/17 TEMPLEUX.	No. 4 Section relieved No 2 Section who returned to Headquarters ROISEL.	

Army Form C. 2118.

WAR DIARY Cadenet 469th Field Co. R.E.
or
INTELLIGENCE SUMMARY. 1st to 30th April 1917.

(Erase heading not required.)

Instructions regarding War Diaries and Intelligence Summaries are contained in F.S. Regs., Part II and the Staff Manual respectively. Title pages will be prepared in manuscript.

Hour, Date, Place	Summary of Events and Information	Remarks and references to Appendices
29/4/17. TEMPLEUX.	No 2 Section proceeded to TEMPLEUX relieving No 4 Section who returned to ROISEL	
30/4/17 HESBECOURT.	No 1 Section proceeded to HESBECOURT relieving No 3 Section who also returned to ROISEL	
1/4/17 to 30/4/17 ROISEL.	Company less 2 sections employed on Road Cuttings, Repairing Roads, Construction of Support & Intermediate line Eastern of Adrian Huts. ROISEL & HAMELET. Wiring ROISEL etc.	

W.R. James Major C
o/c 469th FIELD Co
R.E.

Forms/C. 2118/10.

• ORIGINAL.

WAR DIARY of 469th FIELD Co. R.E.

INTELLIGENCE SUMMARY. from 1st to 31st May 1917.

(Erase heading not required.)

Army Form C. 2118.

Hour, Date, Place	Summary of Events and Information	Remarks and references to Appendices
1/5/17 to ROISEL	Two sections worked continuously on FRONT LINE system attached to BRIGADES. Work: Constructing Fire Trenches, Wire Entanglements, Observation Posts, Shelters etc. Remainder of Company Employed on SUPPORT LINE, also Erecting Elephant Shelters, Aaron Huts, Repairing Roads, Filling in Mine Craters, assisted in Wiring Forward Posts.	Vol 4
ROISEL 29.5.17 NEUVILLE 2.30 AM	Nos 1, 3 & 2 Sections Company marched to NEUVILLE. Headquarters at P.22.d.08.55. Map 57C	
NEUVILLE 31/5/17	No 2 Section attached to K.1 Field Company to assist in Construction of Communication Trenches & Wiring.	

M R James Major
O/C 469th Field Co R E

Original

WAR DIARY
or
INTELLIGENCE SUMMARY.
(Erase heading not required.)

Army Form C. 2118.

469th Field Co.
T.F. R.E.

Instructions regarding War Diaries and Intelligence Summaries are contained in F.S. Regs., Part II. and the Staff Manual respectively. Title pages will be prepared in manuscript.

Hour, Date, Place	Summary of Events and Information	Remarks and references to Appendices
Help to 25/6/17 NEUVILLE.	1 Section attached to H.1 Field Co. for construction of tramway and hand pumping communication trenches vicinity BEAUCAMP.	
25/6/17 to 27/6/17 NEUVILLE.	1 Section employed on usual CABLE SCHEME in forward area	
28/6/17 to 30/6/17 NEUVILLE.	Remainder of Company employed during the week as follows:— Re-work a) Construction - Baths & Divisional area b) " - Officers & Communication latrines c) " - Strong points & dug-outs d) Repairs - made on Linters e) Erection - Adrian huts f) Paving - Horse Watering troughs g) Construction - Prisoners Cage METZ h) Repairing - new Camps Divisional area	J. Annis Major O.C. R.E. 469th Field Co. R.E.

ORIGINAL

Army Form C. 2118.

Vol 6

WAR DIARY
of 469th Field Co. R.E.

INTELLIGENCE SUMMARY.
(Erase heading not required.)

from 1st to 31st July 1917

Instructions regarding War Diaries and Intelligence Summaries are contained in F.S. Regs., Part II. and the Staff Manual respectively. Title pages will be prepared in manuscript.

Hour, Date, Place	Summary of Events and Information	Remarks and references to Appendices
1/7/17 to 5/7/17. Neuville.	Company employed on R.E. work in Divisional Area (as enumerated in War Diary for June 1917)	
6/7/17 BARASTRE.	No. 1 & 3. Sections proceeded to BARASTRE & commenced erection of Lieut. H.Q. Brigade Baths & Camp and Company Camp in new Area.	
10/7/17 BARASTRE.	Coy. H.Qrs. & No. 2 & 4 Sections removed to BARASTRE.	
10/7/17 to 14/7/17. BARASTRE.	Company employed on following work in new Area. Erection of Div. Hqrs. " " 177th Brigade Camp. " " " Baths. " " Company Camp.	
15/7/17 to 31/7/17. BARASTRE.	Company Training carried out while Division was "out of the Line."	
27/7/17 LE. TRANSLOY.	Divisional Field Day. Company forming strong points, wire entanglements, C.T.s etc.	(Sgd) N H Barned Captⁿ N H Barned Captⁿ O/C 469 Fd Co RE a/9. 0/c 469

ORIGINAL.

WAR DIARY
of 469TH FIELD Coy. Army Form C. 2118.
or R E
INTELLIGENCE SUMMARY.
(Erase heading not required.) From 1ST to 31ST AUG 1917.

Instructions regarding War Diaries and Intelligence Summaries are contained in F.S. Regs., Part II and the Staff Manual respectively. Title pages will be prepared in manuscript.

Hour, Date, Place	Summary of Events and Information	Remarks and references to Appendices
1ST to 21ST AUG 1917. BARASTRE	Company. Employed on Construction of Winter Camp. O.16 Central, Erection of Nissen Huts, Wiring, Shelters, Park Horse Standings etc.	Vol 7
.8.17. BARASTRE.	DIVISIONAL FIELD DAY. Company employed on Consolidation & construction of STRONG POINT.	
.8.17. BARASTRE.	BRIGADE FIELD DAY. 2 Sections Sappers attached	
.8.17. BARASTRE.	Inspection of Divisional RE. FIELD COMPANIES by G.O.C. 59TH DIV	
.8.17 MILLENCOURT.	Company marched to MILLENCOURT.	
.8.17 to .8.17 MILLENCOURT.	Company training carried out	

M. Jones Major
OC 469th FIELD Coy
the FIELD R.E.

96MMh.

WAR DIARY
or
INTELLIGENCE SUMMARY.

Army Form C. 2118.

469th FIELD COY. R.E.

Sept 1st to 30th 1917.

(Erase heading not required.)

Instructions regarding War Diaries and Intelligence Summaries are contained in F.S. Regs., Part II. and the Staff Manual respectively. Title pages will be prepared in manuscript.

Hour, Date, Place	Summary of Events and Information	Remarks and references to Appendices
10.30 AM. 1.9.17. MILLENCOURT	Company marched from MILLENCOURT to ALBERT. Entrained for PROVEN.	
10 PM. " PROVEN.	Company detrained & marched to OUDEZEELE. 2/Lt WILCOX sustained bruises and abrasions during railway journey.	
2.9.17. OUDEZEELE.	Company carried on training.	
3.9.17. "	2/Lt WILCOX evacuated to C.C.S.	
6 AM 4.9.17. "	Sappers went to POPERINGHE by Motor Buses. Transport " " " by road.	
4.9.17. POPERINGHE.	Company & transport at HOP FACTORY. Officers Headquarters 129 RUE d'YPRES.	
5.9.17. "	Sappers employed repairing huts.	
6.9.17. "	Company attached to 5th Corps workshop. except C.M.E. & 5th Corps traffic.	
"	Employed on Corps workshops & preparing Siege Bunks, carried on by Coy.	
8.9.17 "	Company employed making road Convent Houses Camp.	

Army Form C. 2118.

WAR DIARY
or
INTELLIGENCE SUMMARY.

469th Field Co. R.E.   Sept 1st to 30th 1917

(Erase heading not required.)

Instructions regarding War Diaries and Intelligence Summaries are contained in F. S. Regs., Part II. and the Staff Manual respectively. Title pages will be prepared in manuscript.

Hour, Date, Place	Summary of Events and Information	Remarks and references to Appendices
1/9/17 POPERINGHE	Company employed at R.E. Workshops & Construction of Remount Laying Camp. O.P. for H.A.	Ml
8.9.17 "	Demonstration of Standard wire Entanglements carried out at Capt H.R. Wise by 20 an Standard pattern for Corps	Ml
9.9.17 "	Entered into Remount Laying Camp at " " Banbury road of Camp	Ml Ml Ml
2 " 17	Company Company entrained for Ypres	
23/9/17 YPRES	Company marched to YPRES. Headquarters & billets situated at 53 RUE DIXMUDE, YPRES. Transport at DIXMERTINGHE.	Ml
	Sappers commenced work on Mule & Duck Board Track No.5 leading from YPRES via BANK FARM to HILL 37. 230 yards track laid.	Ml
24.9.17 YPRES	All Sections continued work on track 406 yards laid.	Ml

(73989) W4141—463. 400,000. 9/14. H.&J.Ltd. Forms/C. 2118/10.

Instructions regarding War Diaries and Intelligence
Summaries are contained in F.S. Regs., Part II.
and the Staff Manual respectively. Title pages
will be prepared in manuscript.

WAR DIARY 4/9th Reg't Field C. Pk. O.E.
or
INTELLIGENCE SUMMARY. Sept 1st to 30th 1917.

(Erase heading not required.)

Army Form C. 2118.

Hour, Date, Place	Summary of Events and Information	Remarks and references to Appendices
25.9.17. YPRES	4 Sectg cacks (old German Concrete Shelters) strengthened & cleaned out for Brigade H.R. Entrances were secure from Shell fire. Map Ref. C.24.c.3.6. Show carried to forward area?	
26.9.17 YPRES	ATTACK made by 59th Division in conjunction with Divisions on right & left. To 3 & 4 Sections attached to 177th Brigade for making Strong Points at DOUCHY FARM. & twenty three Sections went in forward with advancing party. 5.00 non Sect at 4.0 AM. vicinity DELVA FARM. at 4.30 AM. These Sections were supposed to ready by Enemy bombardment 8 Suffered following casualties:—	
	Officers Killed II Lt P. M. LABDON.	
	Wounded II Lt B. ROYEE.	
	Other Ranks Killed Lt Col G. N. STAILEY	
	Wounded Sgt. A. KING	
		Sgt J. HEMMINGSLEY.
		6 Sappers

WAR DIARY 469th Field Co RE
or
INTELLIGENCE SUMMARY. Sept 1st to 30th 1917

Army Form C. 2118.

(Erase heading not required.)

Hour, Date, Place	Summary of Events and Information	Remarks and references to Appendices
26.9.17. YPRES.	Section returned in fatigue until 12.10 P.M. when men were received from G.O.C. 177th Brigade to go forward. C.S.M. WAITE J. was allotted to the party, apparently with the remainder of the 2 Sections to DOUCHY FARM. Slightly looking fairly away the Instructions were received & could not accept any Officers all the material collected for Demolition had been blown to bits. On arrival at DOUCHY FARM. C.S.M. Waite reported to Col RUPPEY. 5th LINCOLN'S. The party remained in vicinity for 2 hours but the situation did not permit of any further work being done. They then returned to OAK FARM. 2 more. employed in repairing Brigade H.R.	

WAR DIARY or INTELLIGENCE SUMMARY.

469th Field Co. R.E.

Sept 1st to 30th 1917

Army Form C. 2118.

(Erase heading not required.)

Hour, Date, Place	Summary of Events and Information	Remarks and references to Appendices
26.9.17. YPRES	which had been badly shelled. No 1 & 2 Sections employed on extension of Right of Mule Track Road track. They were in position OLD BRITISH FRONT LINE TRENCH supply at 4.0 A.M. & commenced work at 5.50 A.M. forming the front. The track which was being filled & obliterated in places was kept open throughout the duration of the advance to HILL 35 & went on as far as HILL 37. Sections were relieved at 5.0 P.M. by Pioneer Company & returned to billets. Casualties for No 1 & 2 Sections 6 other ranks wounded —	

WAR DIARY *Hq 4th Field Co N.Z.*
or
INTELLIGENCE SUMMARY. *Sept 17th to 30th 1917*

Army Form C. 2118.

(Erase heading not required.)

Instructions regarding War Diaries and Intelligence Summaries are contained in F. S. Regs., Part II. and the Staff Manual respectively. Title pages will be prepared in manuscript.

Hour, Date, Place	Summary of Events and Information	Remarks and references to Appendices
27.9.17 YPRES.	8.0 A.M. All Sappers continued on repair & extension of No 5 track - relieved at 6.0 P.M. by Pioneer Bn.	Ypl.
28.9.17 "	Not worked on No 5 track. Reconns got out for 6. Bty Elephant shelters on BANK FARM. (C. 24 b. Central)	Ypl.
29.9.17 "	Sappers day & night shifts on shelters 2 day shift on track. (No 5) 6 Elephant (Bty) Shelters completed today. Foggy & made photography on nights 29/30.	Ypl.
11.0 AM 30/9/17 " VLAMERTINGHE	Company relieved by 4th FIELD Co. NEW ZEALAND Dm NE. Transport lines shifted to Aa road. Casualties 16 HORSES Killed & 6 wounded.	Ypl.

WAR DIARY 469th Field Co RE Army Form C. 2118.
or
INTELLIGENCE SUMMARY. Sept 1st 1917 to Sept 30th 1917

(Erase heading not required.)

Hour, Date, Place	Summary of Events and Information	Remarks and references to Appendices
11.0 AM 3/9/17 YPRES. VLAMERTINGHE	Sappers moved into tents at VLAMERTINGHE.	Nil.
" VLAMERTINGHE.	Transport moved by road to WATOU (Area No 1)	Nil.

W. James Major
469 th Field Co RE
OC 469th Field Co RE

ORIGINAL

Vol 9

WAR DIARY of 469th FIELD Cº R.E.
INTELLIGENCE SUMMARY
(Erase heading not required.) FROM 1st to 31st OCTOBER, 1917

Army Form

Instructions regarding War Diaries and Intelligence Summaries are contained in F.S. Regs, Part II. and the Staff Manual respectively. Title Pages will be prepared in manuscript.

Place	Date	Hour	Summary of Events and Information	Remarks and references to Appendices
MERTINGHE	1-10-17	8·30 a.m.	Sappers marched to WATOU (Area Nº 1)	#A3.
ATOU	2-10-17	12·30 p.m.	Company, including Transport, marched to SEATON STAGING CAMP Nº 2. Arrived at 3 p.m. and accommodated in French Shelters	M.A3.
			I Lieut: F.R.B. Whitehouse arrived from R.E. Base Depôt.	
ATON CAMP	4-10-17	9 A.M.	Sappers proceeded by Motor Omnibus to THIENNES. Arrived 2 p.m.	M.A3.
		11. A.M.	Transport travelled by road to CAISTRE.	
			I Lieut: H.S. Couch-Johns arrived from R.E. Box Depôt	
IENNES	5.10.17	3·30 p.m.	Transport arrived at THIENNES.	M.A3.
	6.10.17	8 A.M.	Company travelled to EUHEM. Half journey marched & half journey by Motor Lorry.	M.A3.
HEM.	7th to 9th Oct.		Sappers carried out Box Respirator Drill, Rifle Practice, Physical Exercises etc.	M.A3.
	10.10.17	9 A.M.	Proceeded by route march to DIEVAL. arriving 1·30 p.m.	M.A3.
EVAL	11.10.17	1 p.m.	Company marched to MAISNIL-LES-RUITZ.	M.A3.
NIL-LES-RUITZ	12.10.17	9 a.m.	O/C & 6 Senior N.C.Oˢ proceeded as Advance Party to AVION SECTOR to take over from 3rd Field Cº CANADIAN ENGINEERS. Remainder of Cº proceeded by route march to VANCOUVER CAMP. arriving 3·30 p.m.	M.A3.

WAR DIARY
or
INTELLIGENCE SUMMARY
(Erase heading not required.)

Army Form C. 2118

Instructions regarding War Diaries and Intelligence Summaries are contained in F. S. Regs., Part II. and the Staff Manual respectively. Title Pages will be prepared in manuscript.

Place	Date	Hour	Summary of Events and Information	Remarks and references to Appendices
VANCOUVER CAMP	13.10.17	7.A.M.	Nos 2 & 4 Sections, in charge of 2nd Lieut. C.L. BRONSDON & 2nd Lieut. H.S. COUCH-JOHNS marched to AVION SECTOR to relieve 3rd FIELD Co C.E. Forward Co Headquarters at S.16.a.1.8.	M.M.B.
		9.A.M.	Remainder of Co with Transport proceeded to ABLAIN ST. NAZAIRE. Co Headquarters X.10.b.0.2.	M.M.B.
AVION SECTOR	17.10.17		No 3. Section, in charge of 2nd LIEUT. F.R.B. WHITEHOUSE proceeded to FORWARD AREA.	M.M.B.
"	19.10.17		No 1 Section in charge of LIEUT. K.G. GRIFFITHS relieved No 4 Section in Do.	M.M.B.
ABLAIN ST NAZAIRE	19.10.17	12.	Reinforcements arrived from R.E. Base Depôt.	M.M.B.
"	22.10.17	10.	N.C.O.s do do	M.M.B.
AVION SECTOR	23.10.17		No 4. Section relieved No 2. Section	M.M.B.
BOUCHIN	24.10.17	7.A.M.	2nd LT. C.L. BRONSDON & 5 N.C.O.s proceeded by motor bus to FIRST. ARMY. MINE SCHOOL.	M.M.B.
AVION SECTOR	30.10.17		No 2. Section relieved No 1 Section.	M.M.B.
	14th to 31st		Three Sections employed supervising night & day Inf: Working Parties upon the following work. Clearing, deepening, widening, draining, laying single & double duck board tracks, clearing & remaking firm. C.T.s & Fire Trenches. Fixing "A" Frames & revetting with hurdles.	M.M.B.
M. d. 4. 9.			Repairs & additions to deep dug-out to make same accommodate 2. R.E. Sections. Constructing M.G. Emplacements.	

N.W. Bowood Capt.
O/C. 69th Field Coy R.E.
July O/C. 69th Field Coy R.E.

1875 Wt. W593/826 1,000,000 4/15 J.B.C. & A. A.D.S.S./Forms/C. 2118.

WAR DIARY

of

INTELLIGENCE SUMMARY.

469th Field Coy R.E.

Army Form C. 2118.

(Erase heading not required.) from 1st to 30th November 1917.

Hour, Date, Place		Summary of Events and Information	Remarks and references to Appendices
1.11.17	AVION SECTOR (LENS)	Company employed on trench system.	Vol 10
17.11.17	"	Training opening OT's & fire trenches	
18.11.17	"	Machine Gun positions. Dug outs etc.	
19.11.17	AGLAIN St NAZAIRE	No 4. Section entrained 10 Gas casualties (slight)	
19.11.17	GOUY en A.	Company relieved by 3rd Field Coy (aus engineers)	
20.11.17	RANSART.	Company marched to GOUY. EN ARTOIS	
22.11.17	ACHIET LE PETIT.	" " RANSART.	
23.11.17	DESSART WOOD.	" " ACHIET LE PETIT.	
		Officers entrained for FINS. marched to DESSART WOOD CAMP.	
24.11.17	DESSART WOOD.	Company marched to COOGECOURT. erected R E camp & started erection of Infantry camps.	

Army Form C. 2118.

WAR DIARY
or
INTELLIGENCE SUMMARY.
(Erase heading not required.)

Instructions regarding War Diaries and Intelligence Summaries are contained in F.S. Regs., Part II. and the Staff Manual respectively. Title pages will be prepared in manuscript.

Hour, Date, Place	Summary of Events and Information	Remarks and references to Appendices
TRESCAULT. 28.11.17	Company marched to TRESCAULT.	W/
29.11.17	Erected tents for Adv. Div. H.Q.	W/
"	Company marched to FLESQUIERES & immediately proceeded to work on defences of FLESQUIERES.	W/

M.R. James Major
1st Field Coy R.E.
O/C H69

Original

Army Form C. 2118.

WAR DIARY of 469th Field Coy R.E.
or
INTELLIGENCE SUMMARY.
(Erase heading not required.) From 1st to 31st Dec 1917.

Hour, Date, Place	Summary of Events and Information	Remarks and references to Appendices
3.0 A.M. 1.12.17. FLESQUIERES.	Coy arrived at FLESQUIERES. Billeted in cellars	
" 1.12.17.	Constructed system of front & support line	
" 10.12.17.	trenches in front of village extending as Reserved line. & using semi-circular by Infantry Working Parties	
" 7.12.17.	Lt K.C. GRIFFITHS. wounded in arm & evacuated to hospital	
" 8.12.17.	" 2 Lt R.B WHITEHOUSE. slightly wounded & evacuated	
" 8.12.17	Lt H.S. COUCH. JOHNS / Evacuated sick	
{ 1.12.17. { 10.12.17	9. Sappers wounded. 8 evacuated during this period	
" 9.12.17.	No 1 Section withdrawn to TRESCAULT. to construct Dug outs at Brigade Headquarters.	

WAR DIARY of 469th Field Coy. R.E.
or
INTELLIGENCE SUMMARY from 1st to 31st Decr 1917.

Army Form C. 2118.

(Erase heading not required.)

Instructions regarding War Diaries and Intelligence Summaries are contained in F. S. Regs., Part II. and the Staff Manual respectively. Title pages will be prepared in manuscript.

Hour, Date, Place	Summary of Events and Information	Remarks and references to Appendices
FLESQUIERES. 10.12.17	Coy relieved on front line by 470th Field Coy.	WJ
GRAND RAVINE 10-12-17	Coy moved into Bivy Outs about 1 mile behind FLESQUIERES. to vicinity of GRAND RAVINE.	WJ
FLESQUIERES. 10/12/17 to 22/12/17	Coy cleared & deck loaded main Communication Trenches leading into FLESQUIERES.	WJ
	Wired & prepared BILHEM. CHAPEL. WOOD. SWITCH TRENCH. for defence	WJ
	Removed Enemy wire from UNSEEN. SUPPORT. TRENCH.	WJ
23.12.17	Coy relieved by 93rd FIELD COY. R.E.	WJ
ROCQUIGNY. 23.12.17. 7.0 pm.	Marched to rest billets ROCQUIGNY.	WJ
24.12.17	TRANSPORT. proceeded by road to SARS LE BOIS.	WJ
NEUVILLE 20.12.17 7.30 AM.	LT A.T.PARKER & LT J.LEWIS arrived at NEUVILLE. Horses Lines	WJ

(0 29 6) W 3332—1107 100,000 10/15 H W V Forms/C: 2118/10.

Army Form C. 2118.

WAR DIARY
or
INTELLIGENCE SUMMARY.
(Erase heading not required.)

469th Field Coy R.E.
from 1st to 31st Decr 1917.

Hour, Date, Place	Summary of Events and Information	Remarks and references to Appendices
ROCQUIGNY. 7.30 A.M. 25.12.17.	Coy. (dismounted) marched to BAPAUME. Entrained for FREVENT. for SARS LE BOIS	A.R.1
SARS LE BOIS. 4.0 P.M. 25.12.17.	Coy arrived SARS LE BOIS.	A.R.2
" 7.0 " "	" transport arrived do.	
do 26.12.17	} Coy Training.	A.R.3
" 31.12.17		A.R.4
do 27.12.17	Lt E.E. ROUSE. joined Coy from R.E. Base	A.R.5
do 31.12.17 2.30 P.M.	Coy marched into new billets at REBREUVIETTE.	A.R.6

W.R. Jenks Major
OC 469th Field Coy R.E.
31/12/17

Original

WAR DIARY
of 469th Field Co. R.E.
INTELLIGENCE SUMMARY. From 1st January 1918 to 31st January 1918.

Army Form C. 2118.

(Erase heading not required.)

Hour, Date, Place	Summary of Events and Information	Remarks and references to Appendices
1-1-18. REBREUVIETTE.	3 Reinforcements arrived from R.E. Base Depot.	WB.
2-1-18 do	Sappers repairing billets of 177th Infantry Brigade at villages of PENIN. AMBRINES. LIGNEREUIL.	WB.
3-1-18 do	No. 3 Section Officer proceeded on leave to U.K. for 14 days.	WB.
5-1-18 do	O/C. 1 & 2 Section Officers engaged in 177th Brigade Exercise	WB.
6-1-18 do	1 N.C.O rejoined from R.E. Base Depot	WB.
7-1-18 do	1 Sergt & 8 Sappers proceeded to PENIN to repair billets for Infantry (177th BRIGADE)	WB.
	2 Sections - Musketry Practice DENIER. Rifle Range	
11-1-18 do	No. 1 Section Officer to U.K. for 14 days leave.	WB.
15-1-18 do	Nos. 3 & 4 Sections. Musketry Practice DENIER.	WB.
18-1-18 do	O/C B° proceeded on leave to U.K. for 15 days.	WB.
21-1-18 do	Captn M. A. Boswell returned to B° upon completion of 3 weeks Instructional Course at R.E. School G.H.Q.	WB.
	No. 3 Section Officer returned from leave to U.K	
22-1-18 do	5 Reinforcements arrived from R.E. Base Depot	WB.
	Company Horses inspected by D.A.D.V.S	
25-1-18 do	5 Reinforcements arrived from R.E. Base Depot.	WB.

Army Form C. 2118.

WAR DIARY
or
INTELLIGENCE SUMMARY.
(Erase heading not required.)

Instructions regarding War Diaries and Intelligence Summaries are contained in F.S. Regs., Part II. and the Staff Manual respectively. Title pages will be prepared in manuscript.

Hour, Date, Place	Summary of Events and Information	Remarks and references to Appendices
27-1-18 REBREUVIETTE	No 1. Section Officer returned from leave. Instructions received for Co. to proceed to ERVILLERS on 29/30 Janry with.	with.
29-1-18 do	Company proceeded by route march to BERLES-AU-BOIS.	ditto.
30-1-18 BERLES-AU-BOIS.	Saffels marched to ERVILLERS. Transport remained behind at BERLES-AU-BOIS.	ditto.
31-1-18. ERVILLERS.	Work commenced repairing Huts & erecting Stables upon Camps in Vicinity under C.R.E. 40th Div:-	with.
1-1-18 to 26-1-18. } REBREUVIETTE.	Sappers were engaged upon the following work. Repair of Billets in 177th INFANTRY BRIGADE AREA. " " Rifle Range. DENIER. " " R.F.A. " " Billets for R.F.A. Instructing Infantry N.C.O's in Wiring, Revetting etc. Company Training, Sections etc.	

M. Donnell Lt.
O/C. 49
aig

Original

Army Form C. 2118.

WAR DIARY of 469TH FIELD COY. R.E.
INTELLIGENCE SUMMARY.
(Erase heading not required.) From 1ST to 28TH FEB 1918.

Instructions regarding War Diaries and Intelligence Summaries are contained in F.S. Regs., Part II. and the Staff Manual respectively. Title pages will be prepared in manuscript.

Vol /3

Hour, Date, Place	Summary of Events and Information	Remarks and references to Appendices
1.2.18 to 5.2.18. ERVILLERS.	Company attached to 40th Divn. Work carried on on — DYSART CAMP. DIAMOND SIDINGS. NORTH MORY CAMP. DIVL BATHS. MORY. DURROW CAMP. Conducting Days Boys Outs for R.P.A.	M.L.
6.2.18. ERVILLERS	LT. A.T. PARKER. with 5 N.C.O.'s. sent as advance party to take over BULLECOURT. SECTOR from 231ST FIELD COY. R.E. 40 Divn. —	M.L.
9.2.18 do	LT. J. SMITH. 2 other ranks sent to Infantry Corps Lewis Army School	M.L.
9.2.18 do	Dismounted Men moved from DYSART CAMP to MORY.	M.L.
	Mounted Section & transport arrived at MORY CAMP.	M.L.

Army Form C. 2118.

WAR DIARY
of 469 HFIELD COY RE
INTELLIGENCE SUMMARY.
1st Feby to 28th Feby 1918

(Erase heading not required.)

Instructions regarding War Diaries and Intelligence Summaries are contained in F.S. Regs., Part II and the Staff Manual respectively. Title pages will be prepared in manuscript.

Hour, Date, Place		Summary of Events and Information	Remarks and references to Appendices
9.2.18.	MORY.	2C Major W R JAMES returned from leave	
11.2.18	"	3 Sections proceeded to FORWARD BILLETS ECOUST.	
		BULLECOURT SECTOR taken over from 231st Field Coy. R.E.	
13.2.18	"	Pontoon & Trestle Bridging Equipment sent to No.8. R.E. Park ARRAS.	
		Sappers left in charge	
15.2.18	"	LT. E.E. HOUSE left Coy to take over One Aircraft Searchlight Section	
18.2.18	"	2nd LT. E.S. MILLARD joined Coy	
18.2.18	BULLECOURT.	One Sapper wounded & evacuated	
22.2.18	MORY.	2 Sappers (Carpenters) sent to 210th Railway Labour	
23.2.18	"	Capt M.H. BOSWELL admitted to Hospital & evacuated to ENGLAND.	

WAR DIARY of 469 th FIELD Coy. RE.

Army Form C. 2118.

INTELLIGENCE SUMMARY. 1st Feby to 28th Feby 1918

(Erase heading not required.)

Instructions regarding War Diaries and Intelligence Summaries are contained in F.S. Regs., Part II. and the Staff Manual respectively. Title pages will be prepared in manuscript.

Hour, Date, Place	Summary of Events and Information	Remarks and references to Appendices
1.2.18. to 28.2.18 BULLECOURT.	3 Sections worked on line :— 1 in back line :— Section changes weekly. General work :— Construction & repairing trenches Wiring. Schemes Water Supply. O.P. ECOUST. Deep Dug Outs. Machine Gun positions Construction Shelters in trenches etc W.R. [signature] Major O.C. 469th Field Coy RE.	O.K.

59th Divisional Engineers

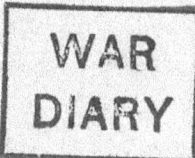

469th FIELD COMPANY R.E.

MARCH 1918

Army Form C. 2118.

WAR DIARY of 469th FIELD COY. R.E.
of
INTELLIGENCE SUMMARY.
(Erase heading not required.) From March 10th to March 31st 1918.

Instructions regarding War Diaries and Intelligence Summaries are contained in F.S. Regs., Part II. and the Staff Manual respectively. Title pages will be prepared in manuscript.

Hour, Date, Place	Summary of Events and Information	Remarks and references to Appendices
10/3/18 to 24/3/18 ECOUST	Company employed on forbattle from BULLECOURT SECTOR. Constructing new trench system. Strongpoints. O.P's Shelters etc.	9D 14
25/3/18 MORY	2 Reinforcements arrived at Coy Headquarters MORY	
12/3/16 "	2 do	
19/3/18 ECOUST	2/Lt J. LEWIS left for England. (LEAVE)	
11 am 24/3/18 ECOUST	Company relieved by 467th Field Cy R.E. Billeted at R.E. Reserve Camp ERVILLERS.	
4.5 am 21/3/18 BULLECOURT	GERMAN OFFENSIVE Commenced with intense bombardment of H.E. & Gas Shells on front & reserve system, followed by powerful infantry attack at 9.0 AM.	
11 am 27/3/18 ERVILLERS	Capt J.S. WILLIAMS reported for duty	

WAR DIARY
or
INTELLIGENCE SUMMARY.
(Erase heading not required.)

Army Form C. 2118.

Hour, Date, Place	Summary of Events and Information	Remarks and references to Appendices
21/3/18. MORY.	2 Sappers and detached party at ECOUST failed to return	M.L
0 P.M. 21/3/18 MORY.	Sappers employed on New Brigade Headquarters MORY.	M.L
0 A.M. 22/3/18 ERVILLERS.	Coy. transport proceeded to CROISELLES LE COMTE.	M.L
	Coy. (dismounted) stood to for 2 hours afternoon	M.L
45 P.M. 22/3/18 do	Employed on ERVILLERS defences	M.L
	Coy. (dismounted) found transport which had moved	M.L
8 A.M. 23/3/18 AYETTE.	from CROISELLES LE COMTE to AYETTE	M.L
30 A.M. 23/3/18 AVELUY.	Coy. marched to BRUCE CAMP near AVELUY.	M.L
A.M. 25/3/18 PONT NOYELLES	" " " PONT NOYELLES.	M.L
A.M. 26/3/18 MONTRELET	" " " MONTRELET.	M.L
0 A.M. 28/3/18 MONTRELET	Coy's transport proceeded by route to MAISNIL ST POL	M.L
do	Coy (dismounted) marched to CANDAS, entrained	M.L
30 A.M. LAPUGNOY	for LAPUGNOY.	M.L
30 P.M. " LAPUGNOY	Coy. detrained, proceeded by Motor Lorries to FREVILLERS	M.L

WAR DIARY
or
INTELLIGENCE SUMMARY.

(Erase heading not required.)

Army Form C. 2118.

Instructions regarding War Diaries and Intelligence Summaries are contained in F. S. Regs., Part II and the Staff Manual respectively. Title pages will be prepared in manuscript.

Hour, Date, Place	Summary of Events and Information	Remarks and references to Appendices
29/3/18 10 AM MAISNIL ST POL	Coy transport proceeded to BETHONSART.	
10 AM FREVILLERS	Coy dismounted marched to BETHONCOURT.	
30 AM BETHONSART	" & horses transport at BETHONSART	
10 AM 3/3/10 "	Coy transport marched by road to LILLERS	

W. R. Lewis Major
O.C. 409 t. FIELD Coy R.E.

30/3/18

59th Divisional Engineers

469th FIELD COMPANY R. E.

APRIL 1918.

ORIGINAL

Army Form C. 2118.

WAR DIARY
of 469th FIELD COY R.E.
INTELLIGENCE SUMMARY.
(Erase heading not required.) From 1st to 30th APRIL 1918.

Instructions regarding War Diaries and Intelligence Summaries are contained in F.S. Regs., Part II. and the Staff Manual respectively. Title pages will be prepared in manuscript.

Vol / 5

Hour, Date, Place	Summary of Events and Information	Remarks and references to Appendices
ST JANTER BIEZEN 1/4/18.	Company (Headquarters) entrained to PROVEN. Marched to School Camp ST JAN TER BIEZEN.	H.W.
do 2/4/18.	Mounted Section arrived at "	H.W.
do	Company inspected by Gen PLUMER—	H.W.
do 3/4/18.	6 Reinforcements received from R.E. Base, Rouen.	H.W.
YPRES 4/4/18.	Company proceeded to YPRES	H.W.
do 4/4/18.	2nd Lt S Eden returned from leave in England	H.W.
	Company attached to 177th INF BRIGADE for work in YPRES area. ZONNEBEKE SECTOR	
do 4/4/18 to 17/4/18.	Construction of Machine Gun Emplacements, Shelters Wiring, Draining trenches etc. Following Bridges were prepared for demolition to stopper back YPRES ZONNEBEKE ROAD Cellars POTIJZE Canreway MENIN GATE	H.W.
8/4/18.	9 Reinforcements received from R.E. Base.	W.L.

Army Form C. 2118.

WAR DIARY
or
INTELLIGENCE SUMMARY.

469th FIELD Coy. R.E.
1st to 30th April 1918

(Erase heading not required.)

Instructions regarding War Diaries and Intelligence Summaries are contained in F.S. Regs., Part II and the Staff Manual respectively. Title pages will be prepared in manuscript.

Hour, Date, Place	Summary of Events and Information	Remarks and references to Appendices
YPRES 12/4/18	Company relieved by Field Coy and Devonn	WL
8.30 pm do	marched to BRANDHOEK.	WL
BRANDHOEK 13/4/18	Capt. L. BUTTERWORTH M.C. Joined Company	WL
3 pm 13/4/18	Transport proceeded by road to MONT DES CATS.	WL
5 pm do	Company dismounted advanced to GODEWAERSVELDE	
GODEWAERSVELDE	billeted at MONT DES CATS MONASTERY	WL
do 4.0 AM 14/4/18	Company proceeded by road to LOCRE	WL
	billeted at MONT ROUGE near LOCRE.	
LOCRE 16/4/18	Company dismounted attached to ROYAL SCOTCH	
	FUSILIERS. To form Mobile Force for defence	WL
do 18/4/18	do Counter attack. Bng 2 Field Sections	
to	line of trenches in front of LOCRE CHATEAU	
19/4/18	2 Sappers wounded	
do 15/4/18	2 Horses wounded by Shrapnel 2 wounded	
	Transport horse heavily shelled	
do 19/4/18	(3 men wounded (2 severely 1 slight)	WL
	5 horses killed	
	3 wounded	

Army Form C. 2118.

WAR DIARY
of 469th FIELD COY R.E.
INTELLIGENCE SUMMARY.

1st to 30th APRIL 1918.

(Erase heading not required.)

Instructions regarding War Diaries and Intelligence Summaries are contained in F.S. Regs., Part II. and the Staff Manual respectively. Title pages will be prepared in manuscript.

Hour, Date, Place	Summary of Events and Information	Remarks and references to Appendices
LOCRE. 19/4/18 6.30 pm	Transport moved to RENINGHELST	WRJ
10.0 pm	Company dismounted marched to RENINGHELST after being relieved by FRENCH DIVISION	WRJ
RENINGHELST 20/4/18	Company marched to BROWNE Camp ELVERDINGHE	WRJ
ELVERDINGHE 21/4/18	do	WRJ
WATOU 22/4/18 to 27/4/18	Defences line constructed EAST & SOUTH of WATOU	WRJ
do 27/4/18	Company marched to ST JAN TER BIEZEN	WRJ
ST JAN TER BIEZEN 28/4/18 8.0 AM	Company marched to find 2 miles south of POPERINGHE	WRJ
POPERINGHE 30/4/18	Company employees with Infantry & Labour Working parties on defence lines	WRJ

Field
30/4/18.

W R James Major
O/C 469th Field Coy R.E.

WAR DIARY or INTELLIGENCE SUMMARY.

Army Form C. 2118.

of 469th FIELD COY. R.E.

(Erase heading not required.) From 1st to 31st May 1918.

Hour, Date, Place	Summary of Events and Information	Remarks and references to Appendices
1.5.18. Billets 2 miles S. of POPERINGHE	Lt H.L.BUTTERWORTH M.C. left Coy. posted to 458 Fielday	MBL
2.5.18 "	Company employed on defences, revetment, supervising Working Parties, sitting of trenches etc	MBL
6.5.18 "	"	MBL
6.5.18 2.0 PM HOUTKERQUE.	Coy marched to SHRINE CAMP HOUTKERQUE.	MBL
10.0 AM 7.5.18 ST OMER.	" Dismounted personnel for ST OMER. Mounted with transport by route NIEUVRELET.	MBL
10.5.18 CAUCHIE d'ECQUES	Coy proceeded by road to CAUCHIE d'ECQUES	MBL
11.5.18 SACHIN	SACHIN	MBL
12.5.18 HOUDAIN	HOUDAIN.	MBL
16.5.18 HOUDAIN.	Coy employed on B.B. LINE Defences Constructing 6 Bridges supervising Work on trenches etc	MBL
21.5.18 FEBVIN PALFART	Coy proceeded by road to FEBVIN PALFART	MBL
22.5.18 PALFART	" " " CLARQUES	

Army Form C. 2118.

WAR DIARY
or
INTELLIGENCE SUMMARY.

469 FIELD COY RE
1st to 31st MAY 1918

(Erase heading not required.)

Instructions regarding War Diaries and Intelligence Summaries are contained in F. S. Regs., Part II. and the Staff Manual respectively. Title pages will be prepared in manuscript.

Hour, Date, Place	Summary of Events and Information	Remarks and references to Appendices
23.5.18 CLARQUES	Coy engaged on R.O. Defensive Line (2 Sects)	MRJ
"	# 2nd M E WEMYSS reported for duty	MRJ
25.5.18 "	# 2 Lt HOLDEN & Lt FINNEGAN reported for duty	MRJ
27.5.18 "	# Lt WEMYSS departed for duty with 2/5 Coy	MRJ

Field
31/5/18.

M R Jones Major
O/c 469 Field Coy RE

Army Form C. 2118.

WAR DIARY
or
INTELLIGENCE SUMMARY.
(Erase heading not required.)

of 469th FIELD COY. R.E.

1st to 30th JUNE 1918.

Instructions regarding War Diaries and Intelligence Summaries are contained in F.S. Regs., Part II and the Staff Manual respectively. Title pages will be prepared in manuscript.

Hour, Date, Place	Summary of Events and Information	Remarks and references to Appendices
CLARQUES 1.6.18	Camp removed to L.23 Central (Sheet 36D)	W.J.
" 2.6.18	/c departed on leave to England	W.J.
" 3.6.18	Lt A.T. PARKER do	W.J.
" 4.6.18	Lt V. HOLDEN reported to C.R.E. BEZINC for duty	W.J.
" 5.6.18	/c returned from leave	W.J.
" 6.6.18	Lt A.T. PARKER do	W.J.
" 7.6.18	9 Drivers received from BASE Depot	W.J.
" 8.6.18	Lt C.L. BROWSDON departed on leave to England	W.J.
" 9.6.18	2 Lt F. EVERITT reported for duty	W.J.
" 10.6.18	BILQUES Sectn of B.B. LINE taken over from 431st Field Coy.	W.J.
" 11.6.18	No 2 & 3 Sections transferred to BILQUES	W.J.
" 12.6.18	Lt A.T. PARKER & Sgt EWING departed to Devil Wood (Instructing on Field Works)	W.J.
CLARQUES & 16.18 to BILQUES 30.6.18	CREPY for duty	W.J.
	Company Engaged on B.B. LINE	W.J.
	TRENCHES	
	STRONG POINTS	
	WIRING	
	BREASTWORKS &c	

W.R. [Signed] Major
O/c 469th Field Coy R.E.
30/6/18.

Original

Army Form C. 2118.

WAR DIARY
of 469 Field Coy R.E.

INTELLIGENCE SUMMARY.

(Erase heading not required.) From 1st to 31st July 1918

Instructions regarding War Diaries and Intelligence Summaries are contained in F. S. Regs., Part II. and the Staff Manual respectively. Title pages will be prepared in manuscript.

Hour, Date, Place	Summary of Events and Information	Remarks and references to Appendices
1.7.18 CLARQUES	10 L.H. Remounts received	J.S.B.
2.7.18 BILQUES	2nd Lieut M.E. WEMYSS attached for duty	J.S.B.
3.7.18 CLARQUES	1 N.C.O & R.E. course of Instruction, ROUEN	J.S.B.
4.7.18 BILQUES	Lt. E.S. MILLARD on leave to ENGLAND	J.S.B.
5.7.18 CLARQUES	2nd Lt. F.J. FINNEGAN do	J.S.B.
6.7.18 "	12 Reinforcements arrived from R.E. BASE DEPÔT	J.S.B.
7.7.18		J.S.B.
8.7.18	2nd Lieut. F.F. EVERITT on leave to ENGLAND	J.S.B.
9.7.18	Lieut. G.L. BRONSDON returned from leave	J.S.B.
	2nd Lt. D. Horace (amphio Establishment) transferred	J.S.B.
22.7.18	25 to telephones exchanged at O.Y. DIEVAL	J.S.B.
P.M. 23-7.18	Lieut. G.L. BRONSDON admitted to hospital sick (temporary dismounted) proceeded by motor lorry to FONTAINES-LEZ-BOULANS	J.S.B.
24.7.18. FONTAINES-LEZ-BOULANS	Transferred (by road) to do	J.S.B.
30.7.18 BELLACOURT	O/C Coy. (Major W.R. JAMES M.C.) J.S.B. H.Q acting C.R.E. BELLACOURT.	J.S.B.
30.7.18 BELLACOURT	7 Reinforcements received from R.E. BASE DEPÔT	J.S.B.
	Lt. E.S. MILLARD + 2nd Lt. J. LEW'S proceeded with Nos 3 + 4 sections	J.S.B.
	to funnel billets to take over huts before informing of R.A.P. DUGOUT	J.S.B.
31.7.18 CLARQUES + BILQUES	company engaged turn hats on B.B. LINE returning PORTUGESE Galery Saties DIGGING TRENCHES WIRING BREASTWORKS ARTILLERY O.P	J.S.B. J.G. Watson Captain OC H.A.Q.E. 3/1/18

WAR DIARY / INTELLIGENCE SUMMARY

From 1st to 31st AUG 1918.

Army Form C. 2118.

469 H FIELD COY R.E.

Hour, Date, Place	Summary of Events and Information	Remarks and references to Appendices
1.8.18 BELLACOURT	LT. C.L. BRONSDON returned to unit from Hospital.	V.S. Apel
" do "	II LT. C.A. PICKERING (from 467 H Field Coy) reported for duty	Wel
" do "	To MAJOR W.R. JAMES returned to unit from Div H.Q. (acting C.R.E.)	Wel
4.8.18 do	4 Reinforcements arrived from R.E. Base Depot	Wel
5.8.18 do	II LT J. LEWIS proceeded with 1 other rank to R.E. School of Instruction ROUEN.	Wel
6.8.18 do	Cpl J.S. WILLIAMS proceeded to ENGLAND (1 months leave)	Wel
10.8.18 do	LT W.H. MILLER attached from 470 H Field Coy	Wel
18.8.18 do	4 Reinforcements arrived from R.E. Base Depot	Wel
20.8.18 do	Sgt J.C. EWING to R.E. Cadet Batta NEWARK.	Wel
21.8.18 do	2 PONTOONS with 1 Sapper in charge to No.5 Pontoon Park	Wel
21.8.18 do	Walkin Trestles & remainder of Coy Bridging Equipment taken over by 470 H Field Coy for bridge at COJEUL VALLEY.	Wel
22.8.18 do	To Coy proceeded on leave to PARIS	Wel
23.8.18 do	II LT W.H. MILLER & 8 other ranks admitted to HOSPITAL (Gassed)	Wel

WAR DIARY or of 469th FIELD COY. R.E.

INTELLIGENCE SUMMARY.

Army Form C. 2118.

1st to 31st AUG 1918.

(Erase heading not required.)

Hour, Date, Place		Summary of Events and Information	Remarks and references to Appendices
1.8.18 to 23.8.18	BELLACOURT.	Coy employed on centre — 3 Sectors in FORWARD AREA deepening widening & duckboarding Main C Trenches. Dug Outs & Shelters	WTL
23.8.18	— do —	1 Section in BELLACOURT on road work. Lullier etc.	WTL
23.8.18	— do —	Coy relieved by FIELD COY. of 52nd DIV.	WTL
23.8.18 — 8.0 pm	— do —	Transport proceeded by road to REBREUVIETTE thence to ANVIN arriving ST QUENTIN 4.30 pm 25/8/18.	WTL
23.8.18 10.30 pm	do	Coy entrained enroute marched to SAVEUTY.	WTL
24.8.18 4.0 pm	SAVEUTY.	Entrained for AIRE.	WTL
24.8.18 12.0 am	AIRE.	marched to ST QUENTIN.	WTL
27.8.18 8.0 am	ST QUENTIN.	Coy proceeded to ROBECQ & relieved No. 5. Coy 7 PM R.E. relief completed by 1 PM	WTL
28.8.18	ROBECQ.	Work commenced on Breastworks (LINE of DETENTION) Bregery RIVER LINE. at B.21.b & B.21.d. Sheet 36.A.S.E.	WTL
31.8.18	— do —	O/C reted from PARIS Leave —	Major

A.H. James Major
O/C 469 th Field Coy R.E.
31/8/18

WAR DIARY 469th FIELD COY. Army Form C. 2118.
or
INTELLIGENCE SUMMARY. R.E.

(Erase heading not required.)

From Sept 1st to 30th 1918.

Vol 20

Hour, Date, Place	Summary of Events and Information	Remarks and references to Appendices
1.9.18 BOISBERG	Lt. G.P.V. GIBBS reported for duty from R.E. Base Depot	Appx
1.9.18	6 Reinforcements received from A.S.C. (3 rode 1.20)	Appx
5.9.18 FOSSE	Company Headquarters moved to FOSSE.	Appx
6.9.18 "	Workshops & H.Q. do	Appx
8.9.18 "	Capt J.S. WILLIAMS returned from leave to U.K.	Appx
10.9.18 "	2 Lt J. LEWIS returned from Engineering Course ROUEN.	Appx
13.9.18 "	Lt. C.L. BROWSDON to Gas Course MAMETZ	Appx
13.9.18 "	3 Reinforcements (rides) from Reinforcement Depot THERUANNE.	Appx
19.9.18 "	14 Reinforcements from R.E. Base Depot	Appx
23.9.18 "	Lt C.L. BROWSDON returned from Gas Course	Appx
25.9.18 "	2 Lt J. LEWIS proceeded on leave to England	Appx
26.9.18 "	Surplus Bridging Equipment Sec 7 from No. 5 R.E. Park	Appx
28.9.18 "	14 Reinforcements from R.E. Base Depot	Appx
1 to 15.9.18	Company engaged during the month on Construction of Div. H.Q. Dugouts. Bullets splinterproof shelters.	Appx
15 to 30.9.18	Course Horse standings. Baths at LESTRUM. RES. BAILLEUL. Repairing & road repairs	

WH James Major RE
O/C 469th Field Coy RE
30/9/18.

WAR DIARY or INTELLIGENCE SUMMARY

Army Form C. 2118.

469th FIELD Coy. R.E.

From 1st to 31st Oct 1918.

Vol. 21

Hour, Date, Place	Summary of Events and Information	Remarks and references to Appendices
1.10.18 FOSSE	2 Lt J. JENNINGS reported for duty from R.E. Base Depot	MeL
400 1.10.18	2 Sections (Lt C.L. BRONSDON i/c) proceeded to forward billets of 469th Field Coy. AUBERS RIDGE took over forward work.	MeL
	CASUALTIES sustained by Enemy Shell fire —	
	KILLED No 268461 Sapper C.E. WALL	
	WOUNDED 1 NCO & 2 Sappers 5 Horses killed	MeL
2.10.18	Capt J.S. WILLIAMS left Company to take command of 546th Field Coy R.E. 73rd Divn.	MeL
0800 3.10.18	2 Lt G.A. PICKERING left for ROUEN (Special Course)	MeL
500 4.10.18	Remainder of Coy with Transport moved to H.35.C. from BOIS-GRENIER	MeL
00 4.10.18 BOIS-GRENIER	2 Sections joined Coy from AUBERS RIDGE.	MeL
5.10.18	Lt A.T. PARKER returned to duty from 59th Divn School (R.E. Instruction)	MeL
8.10.18	2 Lt J. LEWIS returned from leave	MeL
12.10.18	Lt C.L. BRONSDON appointed Captain & 2nd in Command	MeL
13.10.18	Nos 1 & No 3 Sections sent to BAC ST MAUR to prepare for Bridging operations.	MeL

WAR DIARY
or
INTELLIGENCE SUMMARY

Army Form C. 2118

469th FIELD COY R.E.

(Erase heading not required.) From Oct 1st to 31st 1918.

Instructions regarding War Diaries and Intelligence Summaries are contained in F.S. Regs., Part II. and the Staff Manual respectively. Title Pages will be prepared in manuscript.

Place	Date	Hour	Summary of Events and Information	Remarks and references to Appendices
S CHENLETT	4.10.18 to 16.10.18		Company engaged on following work. Removing road mines & booby traps. Clearing roads & mine craters. Construction of advanced battalion billets. Brigade H Quarters etc. Softening 14th Portugese Battn } attached to coy, working on road drainage & B Coy Pioneers } of Quesnoel area etc.	Appx 1 Appx 2 Appx 3 Appx 4
	16.10.18	1900	Bridging equipment taken to LAVESEE. (Nos 1 & 3 Sections moved to LAVESEE	Appx 5
	17.10.18	1200	Coy moves forward to St HELENE. (Orders received to bridge HAUTE DEULE Canal LILLE) making deviations round road craters en route. Bridging operations commenced at 1930 18/10/18. 3 Bridges completed at 0800 19/10/18. Bridge appearance throughout to carry 8 ton load. Completed 1700 19/10/18.	Appx 6
HELENE (LLE)	20/10/18	0700	Company moved to FARM W of TEMPLEUVE.	Appx 7
TEMPLEUVE	24.10.18	1830	2nd Lt LEWIS. delivered all Bridging equipment to 469th Field Coy.	Appx 8
do	24th to 31/10/18		Coy engaged on road repairs. Softening 14th Portugese Battn & 75 Coy Pioneers	

Rnell & Macdonstmt

[signature] Major

O/C 469th Field Coy R.E.

31/10/18.

Army Form C. 2118

WAR DIARY
of 469th (2/1st Co. Y) R.E.
INTELLIGENCE SUMMARY

(Erase heading not required.)

From 1st to 30th Nov 1918

Instructions regarding War Diaries and Intelligence Summaries are contained in F. S. Regs., Part II. and the Staff Manual respectively. Title Pages will be prepared in manuscript.

Place	Date	Hour	Summary of Events and Information	Remarks and references to Appendices
MAPLEUVE	1-11-18		L.D. Home (No 34) Evacuated to M.V.S.	e/7213
"	5-11-18		Lieut G.P.V. GIBBS struck off strength of company (Wounded 31.10.18 whilst attached to 467th Field (2/1 Co.Y R.E.) (Sick) admitted to Hospital	e/7213
"	"		II Lieut J. LEWIS admitted to HOSPITAL (Sick)	e/7213
"	7.11.18		Company relieved 467th Field Cy. R.E. at TEMPLEUVE taking over Bridging pontoons on River L'ESCAUT	e/7213
"	9.11.18		Company moved to ESQUELMES. upon further enemy retirement Bridges over River L'ESCAUT (map ref I14 b.5.3 Sheet 37) Find him transport maintenance throughout scheme	e/7213
"	10.11.18		Major. W.R. JAMES. M.C. (O/C Coy) proceeds to United Kingdom on one months special leave	e/7213
ESQUELMES	11.11.18	1100	Hostilities cease upon signing of Armistice by GERMANY.	e/7213
"	11.11.18 – 14.11.18		Find him transport Bridge maintenance (map ref I14 b-5.3 Sheet 37) Commenced Heavy Bridge at (map ref I14 b-5.4 sheet 37) for 6 Tons dead load.	e/7213
"	15.11.18	0700	Company moved to ANSTAING by march route	e/7213
ANSTAING	16.11.18	0900	Company moved to SECLIN by march route	e/7213
SECLIN	20.11.18		Lieut A.T. PARKER (No 1 Section) proceeds on leave to ENGLAND.	e/7213
"	"		II Lieut J. LEWIS rejoins unit from Hospital	4/7213
"	23.11.18		II Lieut J. LEWIS admitted to C.C.S. (sick)	e/7213

WAR DIARY

INTELLIGENCE SUMMARY

Army Form C. 2118

Place	Date	Hour	Summary of Events and Information	Remarks and references to Appendices
SECLIN	25.11.18		488,366. Sergt GIBSON H.G. (No 3 Section) awarded. MILITARY MEDAL	e/713.
	28.11.18	0830	No 2 SECTION (2 Lieut J. Jennings in charge) proceeded as advance party to new Divisional ARBA. NŒUX LES MINES, & commenced work upon upon 1 billet	e/713.
SECLIN	16.11.18 to 30.11.18		Company engaged upon construction of Baths at WATTIGNIES & SECLIN. Brigade Cement Huts. SECLIN. Education Scheme. etc.	e/713.

2/Lt Brandon Capt. R.E.
Actg. Off. Hq 1st Field Coy. R.E.
30-11-18.

War Diary
— or —
Intelligence Summary

469th Field Co. R.E.

From 1st to 31st Dec 1918.

23

Hour, Date, Place.	Summary of Events and Information.	Remarks etc.
1.12.18 to 12.12.18 SECLIN	Company engaged on filling up Craters for 177th Brigade. Evening concert Hall etc. Education Scheme started	
13.12.18 BRAQUEMONT	Coy moved to BRAQUEMONT.	
14.12.18 "	Employed repairing Batto. Camps	
15.12.18 BRAQUEMONT	MAJOR W.R. JAMES sent to meet from leave	
24.12.18 LIGNY ST FLOCHEL	3 Sections Sappers by lorries to LIGNY ST FLOCHEL	
25.12.18 "	1 " " & Headquarters transport to Camp at NEW MINX.	
26.12.18 LIGNY ST FLOCHEL	Coy employed constructing hardstandings & Staging Camps	
27.12.18 "		
28.12.18 "	22 Miners & 2 long service men demobilised	
29.12.18 "	2nd Lt A. REID reported for duty	
30.12.18 "	Capt. G.L. BRONSDON proceeded on leave to England	Major Jacques Major
30.12.18 "	Lt. E.S. MILLARD " " " "	Capt W.R. Field Coy
31.12.18 "	2nd Lt J. JENNINGS " " " "	Major W.R. 469 F.E.

30/12/18

To DAY
GHQ 3rd Echelon

I herewith enclose this
Units War Diary for the
month of January please.

F N Creenhalgh
Major R.E.
O C 470th Field Co. R.E.

24319

WAR DIARY

469th FIELD COY R.E.

From 1st to 31st January 1919

PLACE	DATE	HOUR	SUMMARY OF EVENTS AND INFORMATION

WAR DIARY.

469th FIELD Coy R.E.

FROM 1ST TO 28TH FEBRUARY, 1919.

PLACE	DATE	HOUR	SUMMARY OF EVENTS & INFORMATION.
	2.11		Company undergoes a Demobilization Employment. No 6 Canadian Hospital
	12.11		Major W R James proceeds to U.K. for demobilization
	14.11		2 Lieut A Reid struck off strength and posted to 3347th E.R.E
	12.2.19		Lieut A.T. Parker to hospital (No 6 Canadian H.pl)
	21.2.19		Lieut A.T. Parker returns from hospital
	25.2.19		30 O.R. demobilized
	28.2.19		9 " proceed on leave U.K.

R J Crowder Capt
CC 469th F Co
R.E.

ps
WAR DIARY

469TH FIELD COMPANY FROM MARCH 1ST TO 31ST.

SUMMARY OF EVENTS.

PLACE	DATE	
DUNKIRK	1.3.19	Company employed on Demobilization Camp, No. 8 Canadian Hospital, Gotheren Depot.
MARDYCK CAMP	31.3.19	
"	15.3.19	2nd Lieut A. REID proceeds on leave to U.K.
"	19.3.19	Information received from D.H.Q. regarding posting of Major R.E. FRYER and 2nd Lieuts to Company
"	20.3.19	Lieut A.T. PARKER proceeds on leave to U.K.
"	21.3.19	Orders received from C.R.E 59th Div: that G.H.Q 3rd ECHELON order company to be returned to CADRE, A.
"	27.3.19	Major R.E. FRYER, Lieut R.H. SKIPPER, & Lieut S.P.F NAILER reported from 547th FIELD Co. RE
"	30.3.19	Orders received from C.R.E 59th Div: instructing troops to dispense & and other Ranks liable for service & Completion to be dispatched to C.R.E. 1ST WESTERN DIVISION.
"	31.3.19	Lieut E.S. MILLARD proceeded to C.R.E.59th DIVISION. to be acting Adjutant.
"	1.3.19	4 Other Ranks demobilized
"	to	" " dispersed upon re-employment
"	31.3.19	19 " " Proceeded on leave to U.K.

P.J. Brunden Capt.
CC. 469th Field Co. R.E.

Army Form C. 2118.

WAR DIARY
or
INTELLIGENCE SUMMARY.

(Erase heading not required.)

460th Field Coy. R.E.(T)

June 1919.

Place	Date	Hour	Summary of Events and Information	Remarks and references to Appendices
DUNKIRK	1/6/19	—	Lieut A.T. PARKER R.E. 7A took over Command of Company from Capt G.L. BROWNE M.C.	
	4/6/19		Lieut L. MEEAD RE & 9 OR knocked in. Reinforcement from G.R.E. knocking Brazens.	
	5/6/19		Lt Col E.G. BROWNE M.C. Demobilized.	
	6/6/19		13 OR. (Class Z) sent for dispersal.	
	7/6/19		G.O.C. the Officers RE & 1 Sgr. departed for furlough (See Gen 2 years unexpired Colour Service) Nominal rolls etc. handed in to Combustion Camps.	
	12/6/19 1000		Company visited by G.O.C. 178 Infy Brigade	
	14/6/19		1 NCO & 1 Sar detach from 141 A.T. Coy. T. Rock for leave taken to Company.	
	16/6/19		Serial numbers given to those (F.33) Having Equipment unfixed by R.E. Officer	

Army Form C. 2118.

WAR DIARY
or
INTELLIGENCE SUMMARY.
(Erase heading not required.)

469th (NM) Field Coy. R.E. (T)

June 1919.

Place	Date	Hour	Summary of Events and Information	Remarks and references to Appendices
DUNKIRK	20/6/19		1 NCO 6 Drivers taken from 879 Coy R.A.S.C. for 141 A.T. Coy. Horses taken to C. R. post	
	21/6/19		Lt. A. F. PARKER, R.E. instructed by C.R.E. Dunkirk to take over temp. command of 225 Field Coy R.E. during leave of the O.C. (on leave)	
	2/6/19		11 Horses belonging to 141 A.T.Coy RE & 9 O.R. taken & temporarily returned to unit.	

Arthur Parker Lt F.R.E.
O.C. 469
O.C. R.E.

77   469 3¼ Coy Ph   59
469 3¼ Coy Ph
Army Form C. 2118.

CENTRAL REGISTRY
HEADQUARTERS
WIMEREUX   WAR DIARY
or
18 JUL 1919   INTELLIGENCE SUMMARY.

Instructions regarding War Diaries and Intelligence
Summaries are contained in F. S. Regs., Part II.
and the Staff Manual respectively. Title pages
will be prepared in manuscript.

(Erase heading not required.)

30
Censor

Place	Date	Hour	Summary of Events and Information	Remarks and references to Appendices
DUNKIRK.	3/7/19		Inspection of Workshops by Heads of Library G.H.Q.	
	7/7/19		Advance Party from C.R.E. Wimereux to report at No. 1 Camp & load vehicles to back.	
	9/7/19		Equipment loaded reported to No. 1 Camp Wimereux	
	10/7/19		Vehicles taken to Docks Dunkirk for Shipment.	
	12/7/19		Lorries, vehicles, at Dunkirk took into barges for shipment to England.	
	13/7/19		Equipment inspected by G.O.C. 176th Brigade in behalf of G.O.C. 59th Div who wished the Officers & men good luck & God speed.	
	15/7/19		Sunday.	
	16/7/19		Coy. are apart for Boulogne for home. Arthur Parker Lt RE O.C. 469 FIELD CO Y RE	

FIN!

WAR DIARY
INTELLIGENCE SUMMARY
Army Form C. 2118.

Place	Date	Hour	Summary of Events and Information	Remarks and references to Appendices
DUNKIRK	3/7/19		Inspection of Earthworks by Director of Works G.H.Q.	
	7/7/19		Advance party from C.R.E. Dunkirk to report at No.1 Camp & send vehicles to docks	
	9/7/19		Equipment & Gear reported to No.1 Camp Dunkirk	
	10/7/19		Vehicles & Crew to docks Dunkirk for shipment	
	12/7/19		Lorry Vickers & Dunkirk docks to Boyen for shipment to England	
	13/7/19		Equipment, Gear & Vehicles by G.O.C. 178 Inf Brigade in chief of G.O.C. 59th who ordered the officers & men to new Huts & good Tunnels having to buy Dunkirk Horses.	
	15/7/19			
	16/7/19		O.C. reports for duty to Boulogne for .... Dunkirk Horses.	

FINI. Arthur Parker Lt RE
O.C. 469 FIELD COY RE

www.ingramcontent.com/pod-product-compliance
Lightning Source LLC
Chambersburg PA
CBHW081451160426
43193CB00013B/2445